CSU Poetry Series LXIV

ACKNOWLEDGMENTS

Thanks to the editors of journals where these poems, some in earlier versions, first appeared:

Alaska Quarterly Review: "What Would Make Me Happy"
Bellevue Literary Review: "Roominghouse"
Black Warrior Review: "My Brother's Galaxie"
The Cortland Review: "The Bulbs"
Hanging Loose: "In the Shipwreck Diner"
Hayden's Ferry Review: "One Day Old Baby"
Inertia: "1970, Port Jefferson Harbor," "What's Worse"
The Iowa Review: "No Homo," "Sister"
The Ledge: "My Mother Hanging Wallpaper"
Lyric: "The Job of Being Everybody," "Your Town"
Nerve: "Sofa-Bed"
New York Quarterly: "The Brother," "New Mother"
Paterson Literary Review: "Gamelan"
Ploughshares: "Highlights"
Poetry: "The First Present You Could Never Remember Giving"
Prairie Schooner: "Smell and Envy," "What I Do"
Rattapallax: "Snowden"
Samsara Quarterly: "College," "Privacy," "Sanibel Island"
Third Coast: "Park Avenue," "The People in My Building"
Threepenny Review: "The Grand Hotel in Cape May"
Witness: "My Bad," "Young Italians," "Expired"

Some poems from this collection were published in the chapbooks *What's Worse* (2001, The Aldrich Museum) and *First Time Reading Freud* (2002, *Permafrost*). "Smell and Envy" appeared in the chapbook *Wherever You Want* (1997, Pavement Saw Press) and also in the anthologies *Urban Nature: Poems About Wildlife in the City* (2000, Milkweed Editions), *American Poetry: The Next Generation* (2000, Carnegie Mellon University Press), *PoetryDaily* and *Poetry 180: A Turning Back to Poetry* (2003, Random House; online at the Library of Congress website: www.loc.gov/poetry/180).

My gratitude to those who helped with these poems: Shelley Stenhouse, Tony Gloeggler, Angelo Verga, Laure-Anne Bosselaar, Kurt Brown, Martha Rhodes, Lee Sakellarides, Peter Murphy, Renée Ashley, Madeline Tiger, Hayan Charara, Ginger Andrews, Larry Hayward, Stephen Dunn and the late great William Packard. Thank you Patricia Smith, Tim Seibles, Billy Collins, Mark Halliday, Robert McDowell, Bob Hershon, Mark Pawlak, Dick Lourie, Ron Schreiber, Tony Hoagland, Baron Wormser, Helen Hulskamp and Alvaro Cardona-Hine, for help between the lines.

Thank you to the New York Foundation for the Arts for a poetry fellowship that helped support the production of this book.

THE JOB OF BEING EVERYBODY

Douglas Goetsch

Cleveland State University Poetry Center

Copyright © 2003 by Douglas Goetsch
Published by Cleveland State University Poetry Center
2121 Euclid Avenue
Cleveland, OH 44115-2214
ISBN: 1-880834-62-6
Library of Congress Catalog
Card Number: 2003111522

The Ohio Arts Council helped fund
this program with state tax dollars
to encourage economic growth,
educational excellence and cultural
enrichment for all Ohioans.

THE JOB OF BEING EVERYBODY

CONTENTS

I

My Brother's Galaxie 3

War 4

Sanibel Island 5

The First Present You Could
　　Never Remember Giving 6

In the Shipwreck Diner 8

The Dialogue 9

Unbelievable Story 10

Your Town 12

The Day Everything Happened 13

First Time Reading Freud 15

Gamelan 17

College 19

My Bad 20

Highlights 21

Sofa-Bed 23

Expired 24

What's Worse 26

My Mother Hanging Wallpaper 27

What I Do 28

1970, Port Jefferson Harbor 30

II

Park Avenue 35

Roominghouse 37

The People in My Building 38

What Would Make Me Happy 40

Smell & Envy 41

Privacy 42

A Horse in a Field in Maine 43

The Grand Hotel in Cape May 44

New Mother 45

One Day Old Baby 46

Christmas 47

A Beautiful Life 48

The Brother 49

The Bulbs 50

Snowden 51

No Homo 52

Print Dresses 53

Sister 54

Young Italians 55

The Job of Being Everybody 56

for Arthur Goldweit & Lisa Denton

My Brother's Galaxie

The stolen records down his shirt
at the Walt Whitman Mall,
the afternoon women in his bedroom,
the sudden conversion, the youth
group packing our living room
to sing for, and the size
of the '68 Ford Galaxie he bought
for coming down from upstate college
just to play church volleyball
Friday nights with a 16-year-old
Christian girl named Amy.
He had to park it on the street
like a truck, because it had no
reverse. I had my own stories,
but it didn't seem like it yet.
I blacked out on beer at
the marching band party and
woke up on Diane Demerest's
mother's bed. See what I mean?
My brother had maps in his head
of every route through the Catskills
so he could reach that girl faster
in that car so big he felt a lag
between when he turned the wheel
and when it drifted into the fast lane,
its long fenders nudging the future.
I couldn't understand how he
got away with never going backwards,
not even when delivering pizza
in Oswego for gas money, while I
was still trying to navigate high school
hallways among the Fuck Yous.
My universe would widen, but
I didn't expect it. The future:
that's where my brother resided,
a year ahead of me, forever.

War

I'd lean back in my father's recliner,
lace my hands behind my head
and think about the future, flat
and blank as the living room
ceiling I was staring at. Someone
who barely cared spread a kind
of sandy gesso across it in half-circles,
then went off to fuck a woman.
Outside, the bay in winter, dark
coppery green beneath an overcast sky.
Some clouds are bigger than three
states combined. I didn't know that,
just as I had yet to learn that beneath
all boredom was war. At 16
I'd driven my father's Plymouth
with no license or destination,
lifted enough weight to have
decent-sized mice in my biceps,
just in case. I had more hair in my left
armpit than my right, which
embarrassed me, and there were scars
on my thighs I didn't know the origins of.
Across the water in a mansion was a girl
with yellow hair and a deep voice.
Months before, I'd walked the beach
to her house with a wish so strong
it made a movie in my brain. But
now, staring at the ceiling, I knew
better. I knew nothing—
like a driver shaking his head to stay
awake at the wheel. Nobody tells you
your war. You just discover one
day you've been fighting it
for as long as you can remember.

SANIBEL ISLAND

In the end, stuffed with Prednisone,
it was seashells Grandma wanted to touch.
Two years indoors, scribbling delusional notes,
oxygen tubes depending from her nostrils,
she had enough wit left to get my grandfather
to take her to Sanibel Island, let her
kneel in the sunset fingering shells
while he sat in the car and cursed this place
with no coffee shop. She had a few moves left—
including a written request for a divorce
and a last squeeze of my hand. My grandmother
didn't particularly love nature. She called
Westchester "The Country" like any
New York Jew. But we all have a right
to go down to the water when we need to.

THE FIRST PRESENT YOU COULD NEVER REMEMBER GIVING

Could be those coils of clay
you stacked on one another,
smoothed with your thumbs,
stuck in the kiln with the rest
of the class, with glaze
that went on mustard yellow,
came out cobalt blue
and you called it
a pencil holder
gave it to your father
and never saw it again.
Maybe that wine bottle
you wound in tape
in a pattern like wicker,
and when that bottle was
wrapped like a mummy
you rubbed shoe polish on it,
then shellac, called it
a candleholder, or a paperweight,
gave it to your father
with a card that said World's Best Dad
and you never saw it again.

The gifts you gave your father
were hard and heavy
because he meant business
in big shoes coming in at night
grunting or waking up
in the morning grunting.
Tugging his shirt, trying to
get his attention you
consoled yourself that one
of those grunts was for you.
It started low in the gut,

the diaphragm did something to it
and up and out it came.
It wasn't bad or good
but it was for you.
You couldn't look it up
in the dictionary, or bring
it in for show & tell,
or put it in your palm
to throw a fastball,
but still it was yours,
yours alone in this world.

In the Shipwreck Diner

My father and I have breakfast
the month after he's left my mother.
We are at the register when
a woman neither of us recognizes,
dirty, drunk, reeking, taps him—
Sir could you give me a light?
My father half turns to her
but freezes, his gaze locked
somewhere in the chrome.
I think of him lighting
Mom's cigarette for years,
righty, lefty, end to burning end,
two at a time in his lips
in the car on the Maine Turnpike.
I fish the lighter from his jacket
pocket and perform this courtesy
for a woman who breathes
a hoarse *Thank you.*

THE DIALOGUE

Like *12 Angry Men*, it began
with a single doubter, convincing another
there's no such thing as altruism, which
is why a man will give a kidney to his brother
but not to a stranger in another state;
why the celebrity with diabetes never
fronts the charity for cancer; and shame
is what gets an old lady a seat on the bus.
Seven boys in a living room one slow summer
afternoon, none with a job or a girlfriend
or a thing to do. Every now and then
someone got up to take a piss or check
on the demise of the Yankees, returning
to the dialogue, where the twins Rich
and Rob still clung to altruism
on account of their grandmother's pie
and the movie *Brian's Song*. But soon
it was just one saying, "Then why
would they have a *word* for it if it didn't exist?"
We offered the words Kryptonite and
Spontaneous Human Combustion, and he
gave in, and so there it was before us:
no pure goodness anywhere in this world ever.
"My God!" said Big Al, sounding like
his father coming home to a trashed house.
We dug in our pockets, found enough
for a pizza, gathered around the steaming pie
reviewing what we'd established that day,
in a suburb east of Manhattan, cultural backwater
of malls and cul-de-sacs and Miracle Grow,
but now also The Refutation of Altruism,
something we'd given ourselves, to cite
like legal precedent, and keep alive
that senior year of fake IDs and back seat
negotiations, college interviews, Reagan,
and the assassination of John Lennon.

UNBELIEVABLE STORY

She turned to me and said, "Why did Christ die?"
I hadn't quite yet realized I didn't want her
for a girlfriend, despite her interesting nose

and preference for short dresses. She said it—
"Why did Christ die?"—more like a statement
than a question, which I couldn't have answered

anyway due to complete boredom with the subject
as compared to my fascination with what
she looked like pulling stockings over her thighs,

and whether that thought, that vision,
could get me through all the turn-off
of what came out of her mouth. Lucy Crup

her name was. Christians are as horny
as anyone, though awfully blind to it, which
is why they never suspect Mary of a thing,

though Joseph must have felt differently—
we have to allow for at least *that*, don't we?—
walking ahead of his wife and her child

in his own world that winter night.
I picture him with dark bony brows,
serious, clear eyes, eyes a condor might

fly out of. He is confused and angry
and perhaps ready to convert to Islam
if only they'd hurry up and invent it.

I wanted Lucy Crup ever since she straddled me
wielding sun tan oil, leaning over, the tickle
tips of her long hair on the back of my neck.

Her smooth oiled thighs pressing against me
were the lubricated axes on which I thought
my world could turn, thighs that wouldn't quit,

thighs I walked behind in the halls, stared down at
in the chair next to mine, in the back of Social Studies
where she kept quizzing me about Jesus,

and I kept praying she could be someone
less poisoned by that unbelievable story,
someone who *went with* her body, as I

swear her breasts grew by the day. Lucy
Crup where are you now? Have you
found a Joseph to go with your Jesus?

YOUR TOWN

No one hit the piñata, if you remember
it right. Mrs. Becker had to rip a hole
in it because it was getting late
and the school buses were lining up
on the hill that, when you go back,
isn't nearly as steep as you thought,
though didn't you ride down it sitting
on two skateboards with another boy,
wasn't that boy your brother, and did you
really break your ass-bone as you always recount?
Weren't there far steeper hills in the next town,
and wasn't your town—tell the truth—
not remarkable for much of anything?
The pinch hitter for the New York Mets
who came to hand out trophies to your Little League
was from Levittown, not where you lived.
The high school's best pitcher hated
the coach, transferred, made the minors.
The Broadway actress that lived on Scudder Place
never made it to her first face lift.
The funeral home parking lot was quiet
and busy, but it was never anyone you knew.
Things *happened*, you can be sure of that,
but it just didn't seem that way,
not till the devil worship cult made
national news, and they found bodies,
but by then you'd moved away.

THE DAY EVERYTHING HAPPENED

My mother calls the police on me
because of the volume and proximity
at which I yell at her, after she
bitched at me three weeks straight
in that shack she bought in Crab
Meadow after she split with Dad
and sold the house and gave me
a corner of the basement, a rug
thrown over a clothesline. I rush
upstairs for her pocketbook, dig
for keys, throw her on the bed
when she tries to stop me, drive
off in tears, head to the house
of my high school English teacher
who lives alone. He's not there
but I let myself in the back, help
myself to some butterscotch pudding,
collapse weeping on the sofa where
later he finds me, puts his arm
around me, doesn't ask anything,
throws down a pillow and tells me
to lie on the rug. He's going to
give me a massage, a deep massage,
first my back, then my front,
take off that shirt, take off
your pants, he takes off his,
runs his hands in long strokes
from thighs to navel, tells me
to close my eyes, leans down and
kisses me on the lips, puts his hands
down my briefs and feels nothing
happening, rubs his stiff dick
up against me, checks me again,

I'm still soft, and I think he's
about to give up, when he kisses
me again and tells me to tell him
something, anything. What
do you say to your high school
English teacher on the day
everything has happened to you?
You say Thank you. You accept
his cup of coffee, and when you
pull out of his driveway you head
to the man you spat on months
before, to ask how he ever stayed
married to your mother nineteen
years, and if there's a place in his
mistress's house for you to sleep.

FIRST TIME READING FREUD

My copy of his *Introductory Lectures*
had an odor I couldn't place, an organic,
vaguely fleshy … pulpy … baby wipes-
type smell—though not exactly. At 18
I was having trouble concentrating,
though the words, according to theory
were processing themselves in my unconscious
while I kept track of girls in miniskirts
wafting in and out of Olin Library
like wide-winged tropical birds. I'd glance down
at Freud's bleak head floating on the cover,
half in stark shadow, monocle in place,
then gaze across the room at a Korean beauty
whose virtually flat face had gotten her
some modeling jobs, and covers of her own.
She promised her mother she'd wear pantyhose
every day, to help keep out the boys—
as if we'd get inside by accident.
I put my nose to Freud, bent the spine back
deeper to smell … an infant's soft moist head?
… a mother's breast dusted with talc?

I learned about the promise to her mother
when I pointed to new packages of hose
stacked tall on a chair by her bed.
I don't know how I got into her room
or how Freud's language crept into my head—
superego, pleasure principle,
displacement, latent and *manifest*
and all that ugly Oedipus business—
babies with sex and murder on the brain,
little Viennese girls hard-wired
to admire their first glimpse of *zomething egstra,*

15

yet why hadn't I touched mine till I was 16,
and why did our professor have to tell us
about the woman he saw at Woodstock
lifting her naked baby to manipulate
his penis in her mouth, both mother
and son *cooing*, he said, with pleasure?
Does anybody see a problem here?
he asked an amphitheater full of freshmen.
Manipulate was the verb he used. Spackling
putty—that's what that book smelled like.

GAMELAN

Two of us would shop for the house. We'd each grab a cart
in the mega market seven miles out of Middletown.
Josh headed for the bulk aisle, where a dozen kinds of granola,
one claiming to save the rain forests, avalanched
into your waiting bag. I'd go for vegetables—the one thing
we in our quietly warring house agreed on: salad—
hard to believe in those communal days of college
when we all took African Dance, and some learned the Gamelan,
an instrument which took about thirty people to play,
which was supposed to be an entire town in Java,
and once you began you all had to keep going for three days
or else the women would go barren, something like that.
Men on campus were forming support groups
because the feminists kept calling us Patriarchal Rapists,
and though our mission in life was to be third world,
our refrigerator was divided like Europe:
Michelle kept her sprouts and yogurt on the top shelf;
Charlotte took the door; Josh and I split the bottom shelf;
Matt had no shelf—he lived on peanut butter, jelly and matzo.
Keith the sophomore English major stole from everyone
and left Post-It notes apologizing like William Carlos Williams.
But there, in the checkout aisle, with our carts full
we felt like great communal mothers, Josh and me
among real Connecticut mothers who bought chop meat and
TV Guide and I said, "Guess how much?"
Josh said, "How much what?"
"How much it costs."
"A hundred dollars."
"C'mon, guess a number it could really be."
"A hundred dollars."
The register did its drum roll and guess what:
100 dollars and 0 cents.
We looked at one another and there was ... joy, I suppose,

a little of which we brought back to the house,
calling them out of their separate rooms
where they meditated, played guitar, read Marx,
smoked pot, masturbated, wept, read Marx,
to come put away their groceries.

COLLEGE

I lost a girl in a cornfield. She was
the TA of my first and only class
in women's studies. I wrote something
in a paper that impressed her, something
clever I probably didn't even understand,
some words I threw down and she
wrote that she wanted to talk to me.
She claimed that she had never cut
her hair, which hung below her waist
straight and brown, feathery at the ends,
a missing patch by her right hip
that caught fire when she was eleven.
I didn't learn a thing about women
in that class. The men weren't allowed
to talk, just listen *For Once* to women,
long discussions of how to get rid of
He, why the word *Lady* was insulting,
why *Girl* was worse, why Freud was
evil, why all men were *Oppressors*
just by moving the tongues in our mouths.
I don't know how I managed to get
this tall, slender girl into my car,
a rusted Toyota that rode low to the ground.
She was beautiful gathering her hair
to one side before settling in the seat.
I don't think we said a word when
we got out and waded into that field.
It was fall corn, taller than us. The stalks
had shed burnt parts that crunched underfoot.
We wandered different rows, and soon
lost the sound of one another's steps.

My Bad

Ignore her, they said.
They were veterans. They'd seen a lot
of black kids on the last day of school
pleading with, then threatening their
white teachers, who had pleaded with them
all term to get to class and do their work,
and this girl standing at the gymnasium door
was no different. So I concentrated
on keeping my dribble, hitting
the open man, getting back on D
as she stood there calling *Mista, Mista*;
me running full-court with math
teachers, hairy, angular, bearded, bald,
not one of us a match for the boys who dunked
on the bent rims of her neighborhood.
She stayed in that doorway until I was sure
she was right, that she'd *passed* the class,
that it was my bad—I'd confused her
with another girl when filling out my grades.
She'd be going to summer school
unless I did something then and there.
But I didn't.

I could say I was young,
and maybe I wanted just once to leave
a mistake the way men leave women.
I wanted the truth to go away. I wanted
to play basketball, to get a good look
at the hoop, and when I did, when I
hit the open J that won the game
I looked over and the girl was gone.
Fixed in her mind, a snapshot
of how I run, or fake, the sweat
stains I make on a white shirt.

HIGHLIGHTS

Drunk, her eyes would water and sparkle
and she'd hold my jaw in her palm
as though I were her child or dog, saying,
Listen to me, Douglas: don't dare turn
into one of these aging bachelor teachers.
Then she'd reel off names of half a dozen
doddering men in the physics and social
studies departments who wandered the halls
in stained shirts and chalked-up pants
frayed at the pockets, men first in line
every day in the faculty cafeteria,
men who stared deadpan into the lens
of the yearbook photographer.

Come with me, she said. We took a cab
to her gay guy in the Village. She said
I needed once and for all a decent
haircut. She was first. Barry
put a tight rubber cap on her head
and used a hooked needle to pull
strands of her wet hair through holes
until she looked like a shock therapy patient,
her face pale and tired in the light,
and suddenly she was a woman
twenty years older than me getting
highlights. Though she looked damn
good when it was over, climbing
down from the chair in her red shoes.
We found a bar on Bleecker Street.
She put a hand through my new haircut
while I complained about the girls in American
Literature who were giving me problems.
She said they were in love with me,
and wondered at how blind I was

to miss it. Then she told me, finally,
where she went every weekend: Tampa,
to stay with an auto parts salesman
who paid her fare. A man her age, a man
who used to be married to her sister.

SOFA-BED

My last girlfriend broke my bed. Yes
we were having sex on it, and maybe
you think I was at least half responsible,
but she was the one who liked to drift
up into the corner of the padded back
where she'd spread her arms like a queen,
and all I could think of was the man
who sold me this fifteen-hundred dollar
sofa-bed, warning me never to put
extra weight where the head should be,
which was exactly where our bodies were,
humping the morning, she in her
careless abandon, me unable to get
the octagonal rims of the salesman's glasses
out of my head; she producing
lovely, husky groans, me listening
to the complaining of springs and joints
and hollow chrome. She would have
scolded me for such a concern—
a piece of furniture compared to living
in the moment, the pleasure of a woman,
a woman who was, after all this time,
adjusting me to intimacy, wanting me
to connect and come, though I didn't
see why this all couldn't take place
a few feet down and to the left.
Soon it wasn't happening at all,
and in the end I found I could tell
her everything except this—better
to have her think my head was full
of other women, or baseball, than discover
I was Felix Unger guarding the coffee table,
ready with a coaster to ruin his life.
She left me with a convex bed. I sleep
as though on a boulder, feet and head
lower than my chest, listening to the traffic
on Greenwich Avenue, which never stops.

EXPIRED

My grandfather's phone could
give you a heart attack, the ringer

set to hard of hearing, to scream
over Court TV and Andy Griffith

whistling like a mad tea kettle.
The phone was still on stun

when I rolled to the edge
of the bed, lifted the receiver

and heard the night nurse tell me
he was dead. I was too

asleep to remember exactly
how she said it, just the word

expired, which made him sound
like a 90-year savings bond.

The doctor had given him
at least another week, told me

to get some rest. I slept alone,
shirtless in the bed where he lay

insomniac for decades while
his teeth bleached in their glass.

I gathered socks, shoes, keys
and drove down the dotted line

to the hospital, thinking of his
signature, two big letters trailing off

the check he sent when I was
twelve. One quarter of him

would now be mine, he'd told me
as I spoon-fed him ice cream.

WHAT'S WORSE

There are a lot of reasons why a woman
might be crying in an airport.
She needs to cancel her rental car,
furious that Alamo won't keep the promise
they make in their commercials.
Plus, her father is dead.
She has taken a plane a day too late
and what's worse, she wanted to be late.
The woman is my mother.

She wants to know if she can sit with me
while I wait for my flight out of there.
Her eyes are oiling up with tears.
She is shrinking into a little girl, a knot.
"Please go," I finally say, vicious
as she wants me to be. Then she
hugs me, and here's the worst part:
I don't even put down my luggage.
The weight of the bags pulls my arms,
stiffens me, as she puts her fat little hands
in the middle of my back and presses
her cheek to my locked chest.

MY MOTHER HANGING WALLPAPER

How hard she was trying to line up
the edges and hold them there to slather
on what looked like Cream of Wheat.
I didn't think you were supposed to put
paste on the *outside* of the paper but
what did I know. Dad in the city at work,
us in our new house in Stony Brook,
with enough empty walls and garden beds
for Mom to fix and fuss with to her
heart's content. She must have felt sprung
free of Brooklyn, that crowded world
that bent into the thick lenses of her glasses,
every square of sidewalk conquered and
re-occupied with nothing left for a little
Jewish girl to make her mark. But here
was her new life, and it required wallpaper.
In five months we would host Christmas,
Nana or Aunt Sherry might use this bathroom
and perhaps notice the wallpaper, then later
my mother would mention nonchalantly
that she'd done it. In throwaway jeans
and ripped man's shirt, a Marlboro
dangling from her lips, paste caking
her fingers, she worked and measured
twice, getting the repeated pattern—blue
flowers—lined up, another trip to Rickel's,
forging Dad's signature on the credit slip,
my mother at twenty-six, pulling it off,
rubbing it back, smoothing out the wrinkles.

WHAT I DO

I pay bills the way he did,
checkbook, calculator, roll
of stamps laid out on a Sunday
near the end of the month,
ripping the perforations, stuffing
the trash can with what doesn't matter,
licking envelopes, a tidy stack
of outgoing mail, adding it up
to get the number for the month
which keeps the walls around me.
Maybe he felt powerful, or just
responsible, signing those checks,

sitting hours at his desk, slumped,
his big back to me and the rest
of the house. What I did
was bring him coffee, black
steaming cups burning my fingers
down the long carpeted hallway.
I emptied his ashtray. I put my small
fists in his shoes and shined them.
If there was more to my father
it was in a place I couldn't see,
and now that I'm approaching
the age he was when we stopped

speaking, I'm beginning to get
a hint of him in what I say
when I'm not thinking, a glimpse
of his hairline in the rear view mirror.
Sometimes on the golf course I imagine
he's golfing too, five states away,
studying his ball, waggling the club

three times the way I do, a signature
twist of the back, left hand
up to shade the eyes, and the same
God damn son of a bitch!
when it disappears into trees.

1970, Port Jefferson Harbor

We drove out 25A
through Setauket, down
the slope to Port Jefferson,
a right turn into a lot
where, on the third tier,
like a can of peas high on a shelf,
they kept our fiberglass boat.
They fork-lifted it down,
drove it across the street
and backed it into the harbor.
The outboard motor screamed
like a blender, until you
went numb and forgot it,
then it changed speeds
and you heard it again.
The harbor was murky,
smelling of bilge and brine,
gasoline, fish guts and urine
from the rusted coffee can
in the front hatch where
one of us peed kneeling
with his back to the others.
Beyond was Long Island Sound,
where we'd never go.
I could see Rocky Point,
high and thick with trees,
white mansions peeking
through the green like
canvas behind a painting.
Dad positioned us over
a boiling school of moss bunker.
Bluefish eating them from
below. The bunker practically
jumped into the boat.
He put a fat hook through
the back of one, cast it out
and let it swim. He

worked two lines, crossing
side to side, while Andy
slept cooking in the sun;
I sat under the shade
daydreaming I lived in
a mansion with a big dog;
and Mom—I don't know
what Mom did. It's hard to
believe a decade earlier she
and Dad were strangers in line
at Polytechnic University,
and now we were four people
in a boat that would
go back on a shelf
at the end of the day.
The truth about our family
was like looking directly
at the sun: once
we caught a glimpse we
scattered. Two of us
still talk on the phone.
There's a picture from
the day the bluefish went
crazy: us in a semi-circle
behind 44 bloody filets;
Dad's young face and round
gut in his undershirt;
me with bony shoulders
pulled back, showing my
new big teeth; Andy, chubby,
sunburned and scowling;
Mom half out of frame,
smoking. I don't know
who snapped the picture.
None of us could have
because we were all in it.

PARK AVENUE

The helpless rich were just holes to me,
slots in the shaft of the service elevator
where I'd deliver maids and florists,
testing my bad Spanish as we floated
even with the landings. I emptied
morning trash, mopped the stairwells,
then stalled my elevator on the 13th floor,
sat on a milk crate and read *Moby Dick*,
ruminating with Ishmael in the crow's nest.
That was the back; when you worked the front
you had to stand for hours, touch your cap
and talk to them. Several times a day
you got to see the tall blond nurse
step through the lobby to and from the plastic
surgeon's office, and when she smiled at you
her blue eyes seemed like wealth itself.
The owners gazed right past us, into mirrors
or down at the rugs, three whale-sized
Orientals laid end to end, inspecting them
as we trailed behind to press the button
for their floor and ride with them in silence
in the walnut-paneled elevator, wondering
why they wanted our company—
didn't they know how much we knew about them
just by when they came and left, their visitors,
their trash, packages; magazines
in brown wrappers to Mr. Harriman 12A,
wrinkle cream and Valium to Mrs. Decker 7D,
a quart of Johnny Walker Black daily
to Dr. Niedermeyer Penthouse West?
Did they know how plainly their voices
echoed down elevator shafts when they
spoke on the phone or scolded their maids?
Or were we *included* in their privacy

because they thought they owned us
the way you'd own a parrot, knowing
it sees everything, repeats niceties,
outlives marriages, perched for decades,
sun down, Christmas morning, in the lobby,
bow tie, stripe down the pants, whistling?
Did it comfort them to know their addresses
were lodged in our heads when we went home
to our sweaty lives across the East River
where people got shot and married hairdressers?
The others, I mean—I'd come to New York
for graduate school, and in September, having
relieved each in turn, for the two weeks' vacation
afforded by the union, I said goodbye
to Martin Casey, Pat O'Rourke, Vic Dumbrowski,
Joe Lotto, and the real Tony Curtis—
the doormen of 1150 Park
who drank too much and played the horses,
had thick-as-worms varicose veins
from standing, waiting, waiting, sprinting—
old men in heavy shoes hailing cabs in the rain.

ROOMINGHOUSE

I was staring at a candle when I heard
the man tumble down the stairs and become
the body they came for. Old Mrs. Caruso
and Pat her nephew, also old, climbed up
from their basement quarters, and she gasped,
and he shooed their poodle, Kevin, back downstairs,
and the other men came out of their rooms
while I stood at the flame thinking *Death*
is not so bad, a finger in a pool of wax,
the sirens pulling up outside, the vestibule
flung open to the winter, the quiet while
they worked, pops of static on a radio,
and the quiet when they left, when everyone
went back up to their rooms and shut their doors.

THE PEOPLE IN MY BUILDING

for Marylouise Burke

The people in my building live alone
in studio apartments. Six floors, one
elevator, a basement full of roaches
where I met Diane folding laundry.
She told me that our building used to be
owned by a hospital trustee who rented
exclusively to nurses. One by one
they married off and moved away to live.
A few are left: Theresa in 6D
who returns at noon in surgical scrubs
to walk her blind schnauzer; Jane in 3B
who receives all the queensize catalogs.
Diane handed me her phone number.
I called and got St. Vincent's Hospital.

The tall woman on the second floor
sold everything to move in with her son
in Colorado, where she could breathe the air.
She used to be a Rockette, and she showed me
black and white glossies proving it.
I bought her air conditioner, her blender
and a pair of long nylon stockings.
The small, mustachioed man on the sixth floor
has a mutt named Lady, a Vietnam Vet
sticker on his door, a tiny Puerto Rican
boyfriend who sometimes wears a dress
and turns tricks on Gansevoort Street.
When he forgets his key, we see him
climbing the fire escape, past our windows.

I only hear the gay couple next door
when one of them is shouting from the bathroom.
They talk like married people, which they are.

Ruth, the widow on the other side,
would press an ear to her kitchen wall
and pound in complaint if she could hear
Johnny Carson on my television.
We all hated her, and then she died—
she'd been dead for days, the firemen said.
You can know your building if you're interested
in sadness. Good things probably happen
but they don't seem to make it through
the walls. Sometimes in the elevator
we'll stand together, breathing in silence.

What Would Make Me Happy

I wake up from naps in the late afternoon
and look around my one-room apartment
sad and lost, maybe for what I dreamed
and can't remember, maybe because
the light in the windows is going down
and the A train rattles by seven stories below,
and I know that in the fluorescent lit cars
they are sad. I have seen them
riding with their lives like friends
they have been friends with too long,
the chubby men who don't tuck in their shirts,
the men in suits with folded newspapers,
the women who stare down at their chipped nails
and the clothes they chose that morning
and were seen in all day.

Sometimes I think of the popular people from college
who have married one another and now have double
incomes and kids in Connecticut and D.C.
This according to the Wesleyan Alumni Newsletter,
a document I've gone to great lengths to avoid receiving,
but it keeps coming, and I keep turning
to my year, looking at the names in bold
and what's written—more marriages, more
kids, promotions, Fulbrights. Someone
climbed a mountain, someone made a speech.
Just once I'd like to read about a drug bust,
a messy divorce, a retarded baby.
But what would make me happy
is someone washing dishes in another room
and placing them carefully in the drying rack
so as not to wake me up.

SMELL & ENVY

You nature poets think you've got it, hostaged
somewhere in Vermont or Oregon,
so it blooms and withers only for you,
so all you have to do is name it: primrose
—and now you're writing poetry, and now
you ship it off to us, to smell and envy.

But we are made of newspaper and smoke
and we dunk your roses in vats of blue.
Birds don't call, our pigeons play it close
to the vest. When the moon is full
we hear it in the sirens. The Pleiades
you could probably buy downtown. Gravity
is the receiver on the hook. Mortality
we smell on certain people as they pass.

PRIVACY

Some people hold a secret
like stolen chocolate on the tongue,

lips closed, eyes defiant.
Maybe they will open and snap shut

to give us a glimpse, like a lift of a skirt.
The thing inside might be a cyanide pill ...

the man boarding the plane with bombs
in his underwear; the anorexic, will

and bones, saying to the world
You can't put any of you inside me.

When Brian Harwin put his toy
drill through his sneaker and found

the blood geyser in his foot
he wanted, not medical attention,

but privacy. When those rednecks
wanted to see if a boy was a girl,

Brandon Teena flailed and folded
arms and legs like a crab. *Where?*

the detectives kept asking,
Where did they rape you?

until they got him to say the words
my ... vagina.

What do you have inside you?
What do you know? How many safe

deposit boxes do you require? How
many keys in how many drawers?

A Horse in a Field in Maine

You think I don't know where I am
because I don't know how far the sea is from here,
and the road touching my field is nameless
as are the hills. You have stopped
your car and come to the fence
with your children, calling, holding
pulled-out grass and a video camera.
And you wonder how I live with myself,
old and swaybacked as I am,
flea-bitten, unable to wipe my eyes.
I'm thinking, *I could bite you,*
take a chunk from the arm of this child
reaching for my salty flanks. But
a calmness overtakes me. It always does.
I know my place in this system
of sun and rain, mosquitoes, mud
and dung, some of which I chomp
with weeds whose roots smell faintly of onion
and tell me I'm part of everything,
even as I stand here stamping my hoof,
twisting out of camera shot while
your children point at my scrotum.
I already am the ditch they'll drop me into
whereas your death will require a stone,
and what is written there will not come
close to, will be worlds away from,
pronouncing your true name.

THE GRAND HOTEL IN CAPE MAY

When news comes on the radio
you wake up, think of eggs and almost
love your country. Maybe the road back
to yourself begins with common courtesy,
the Please on the sign advising where
to throw sanitary napkins, the neutral tone
of the newsman designed to offend no one—
you used to mind this, but now you see
there are people in hotels everywhere
and what they need is clean sheets,
heat in the winter, coffee in the morning,
so wipe away the fog, shave your face
and become human again. They don't
know you here, and they forgive you.

New Mother

He hasn't put his hands on her in months,
but now they're finally having the talk
where words don't matter, just the hum
of their voices, like the sea subsiding.
Then she undoes a button of her blouse
and asks if he would like a taste of her.
He's startled by the frankness of the question,
startled more that she knew what he wanted
even before he did. How easily
she cradles his head as he stoops
timidly, unsure of what it means,
afraid, as some men are, of meeting
Mother by mistake in the dark, while she
feels more alive than she ever imagined.

ONE DAY OLD BABY

for Wyatt Domingo Schmitt

A rag of puffy flesh
in blue blankets, sleeping
as only the very young can sleep,
as if under the world, while his mother
tells us the details of her labor—
a cervix stretched unrecognizably thin—
then steps into the corridor to speak
with a nurse, handing him to me.
Life. He breathes the air
as animals do, knowing somehow the world
is his, though he'll forget this
as he grows into his strange name.
I picture him forty years old
in a train station, dusk, steam
of his breath, feeling ancient.
A young woman in a window slides by
and he'd trade the life he knows in a second
to be in that woman's compartment,
accelerating. Gone. He looks down
at his tattered coat. He can't remember
how he got it, or, for that matter,
what became of the sky blue parka
he wore while making snowmen, age 13.
It must absolutely be somewhere—
everything must—but his life is full
of what he can't retrieve, like this
moment, sleeping in a stranger's forearm,
when it is all he is.

CHRISTMAS

for Kathy Calabrese

They pinned a star
to my skull, wrapped me
in a spiral of lights

till I was brilliant, till I was,
they said, the best one yet.
They sipped cocoa

and stared at me
and I blinked and stared
back into the puffy eyes

of Mother and Father,
Sister, made up like a doll,
sucking in her abdomen,

Little Brother, who sleepwalked,
his blanket wrapped around
him like a storm. Each night

he searched the room for gifts,
then curled up at my feet.
He smelled so individual

in his pajamas when
I bent to pick him up
and carried him away.

A Beautiful Life

If I found a cat, one I liked,
I wouldn't post a sign announcing it,
and I'd ignore the signs of its lost owner.
I'd feed it tuna and give it my name.
And if I ever write a novel, it will be
about a man who kidnaps an infant boy
and raises him in a distant small town ...
attends Little League, tells him all about
girls, where rock 'n roll comes from,
sheds tears at his college graduation.
Can you commit one crime, then pay for it
with a beautiful life? That's the question
this novel would be posing. The answer's
complicated, though I think it's yes.

THE BROTHER

Each day in school he reads
The Five Chinese Brothers
and debates which one to be:
the one they couldn't burn,
the one they couldn't suffocate,
the one with the iron neck,
the one that stretched a mile,
or the one who swallowed the sea.

Walking home, he decides
again on the fifth brother,
his head puffed out like a grampus,
turning crimson, holding it all in
for the foolish boy who gathers
fish off the floor of the sea.

When his father gets to his
second six-pack, the boy sits
in the cabinet under the bathroom sink
and listens for his mother
hitting walls. He will watch
through a crack when the man
appears above, undrapes his huge
cock and lets out the sea.

THE BULBS

for Lisa Denton

I wait in the U-Haul with the kids
while she, in my sister's peasant skirt
and her brother's parka, fishes
the beds with a busted trowel,
then her bare hands thrusting, pulling
dark knots from the cold ground.

Behind her, the torched house
where her mother drank herself
to death, where we lived
until it burned. The insurance
bastards, still investigating,
won't pay for a motel.

I honk—*Come on!* She stands
in the stiff wind, which sends
the charred stink over the town.
Now she walks the lawn looking—
not quite down—almost inside
herself for where she planted.

The kids have mourned
their stuffed animals, didn't cry
when the neighbors looted, but
no way will she leave these bulbs,
which have made flowers in two houses,
on both sides of the Hudson.

Finally she comes to the truck,
the hem of her skirt
in her hand, cradling them.
She blinks back tears, climbs
in, slams the door, says
Get this goddamn thing moving.

SNOWDEN

They called it a mountain, but it was just
a hill that took a while to stop—though I
felt brave enough in my sweater at the top,
reading something about God on a plaque
as little girls who'd climbed ahead of me
chased one another through their mother's legs
and stiff old men stood gazing down at sheep
that wove around the lower hills like clouds
that bore their shadows on their backs.
I lay down for a nap, hoping the winds
would do me the small favor of changing
who I was, the way they had their way
with dunes and schooner sails. But all they did
was whistle, tunes old as the hills of Wales.

No Homo

The boys in detention say it like an insurance policy,
as in *Yo son no homo but that nigga was* big!
because if one forgets *no homo* the others pounce—
Aw that's that homo shit!—which happens
sometimes when we're reading aloud and get
to the word *love* or *body* or *swallow* or *bend*.
When they think my pants are too tight I hear
fuckin faggot under their breath, or *Yo I think*
we got a fuGAYzi here. So I go down to the gym
and hit a few shots from downtown to shut
down that homo shit, you might say; let them
debate instead if a *nigga* can braid another
nigga's hair or does it have to be a *bitch*?

When I congratulate Luis on his execution
of the two-no homo sentence—*No homo B.*
but your test was long *and it was no homo* hard—
he cocks his head and looked at me funny.
I don't know what Patrick is thinking when he says
No homo Goetsch but that's a nice radio, but I do know
the small kids say it more than the big ones, and no amount
of no homo will help where some of them are going
to get initiated by someone who's also not a homo—
as if that mattered. Sometimes they come for a kid
in the middle of class: *C'mon Deshawn you goin'*
upstate, and little Deshawn gets a ritual pound
and half a hug from every boy in the room.

PRINT DRESSES

I have always wondered about women in print dresses,
florals that seem to lock them so completely
into their feminine selves, as if papered

behind walls of petals and plumage.
Women in print dresses, in sling-back sandals
in hotel lobbies or cafés, legs crossed

talking to one another, some gesturing
with their hands seriously as though they've
forgotten the whimsy of purchasing

their outfits the season before, emerging
from fitting room stalls on gray winter days
to find mirrors and turn in them,

a pull here, a tug there, a half-spin
to see how far the skirt will rise and swing
while dancing or in the wind—women

who can worry about mortgage rates
and the line of their lipstick in almost
the same thought—miraculous women

who will at the end of the day step
skillfully out of their print dresses—
some will cross their arms and pull them

over their heads! Most will follow
the wash & care instructions. Good women,
voters, consumers, mothers, closet lesbians,

survivors of eating disorders and battering,
now asleep in rooms where flowered silk, draped
over a chair back, almost seems to breathe.

SISTER

Some boys aren't lucky
enough to have one. Mine
taught me girls aren't good
or bad, their shit smells
and as we grew we gave
each other updates from
the other side of the line
she was tracing with hop
scotch chalk and lip gloss.
So much more feminine
than Mom, who wore pants,
didn't shave and would
sometimes turn and ask,
"Where did she come from?"
Dad let her climb on him,
even while paying bills.
She could almost make
him smile.
               In our teens
I thought we were enemies,
but then I felt her hand in mine.
I was walking Crab Meadow Beach,
she'd come up from behind
and we stepped forward
together in silence. That's how
it will be when the woman
I marry steps into my life.
But I'm almost forty now,
and I never had a sister.

YOUNG ITALIANS

Rome could get you tired with all its rock and dust
in layers of centuries that tell you you are nothing.
Tour buses slide in and out of crumbling ruins
which the young ignore in favor of Levis,
cigarettes, loud cars costing billions of lira.
The Romans themselves are handsome, and the men
wear gorgeous shoes to tell you this,
and the women line their lips and cut their words
into red slices of dialect that stir
things you didn't know were in you.
While tourists stand stiff-necked in the Pantheon
young Italians crowd the gelati store across the street
where flavors taste better than their names—
the coffee more coffee than coffee, the banana a jungle of bananas
sweetened and packed on the tip of the tongue.
They don't drink much, don't stay out late at night
because their lives take place in the sun,
and the old will say that's why they lost the war:
they missed the sun and the food, they missed
cruising the magnificent piazzas
calling *Ciao bella!* and *Ma che cazzo dici!*
shaking their upturned hands at one another like figs in the wind.
They don't need history or death. They get their sadness
from the disinterested backs of beautiful girls.

THE JOB OF BEING EVERYBODY

I can't walk a block without putting myself
in each window I see, to live there

if only for a moment, applying wart medication,
watching COPS, or searching for a wife

on the internet. Though all the rooms
in this city add up to one huge vague regret,

I still wouldn't want to miss the surprise
of each particular sadness, to follow

any given subway rider home
to her glass of sherry. When in Rome

I traced the TV wires down from rooftops,
bras and colored blouses in from clotheslines

to the women who would put them on
the next day, kiss a lover good-bye

and drive one of those puny cars to work.
Most afternoons I rode the buses,

past ravishing brides posing for photos
on the *Gianicolo*, high above

the mental hospital, where you could always
jump to your death and land near a fountain.

In *Villa Borghese* I paced those aisles
of marble busts—what I would have given

to be one of those Latin heads, corroding.

•••

There's a window of a room not seven feet
from an off-ramp of the George Washington Bridge.

I wonder who lives behind that soot-caked glass—
a woman who only goes out for prescriptions?

a washed-up soap star from the '70s?
a vigilante polishing his guns?

In the schoolyard on my way to work
it's always recess, and I always stop

to admire children playing, reliable
as birdsong; also the one plastered to the leg

of the teacher's aide, the fat boy ruminating
in the corner, the coke-bottle-glasses girl

trying to turn a jump rope double dutch
while other girls are criticizing her.

I picture her at 35—contacts, short
hair, managing an office, three kids,

the sails of her marriage slackening,
and I wish I could tell her

You were once this girl, and all you wanted
was to jump rope right in the same

cold wind that's blowing now.

•••

On evening walks in Brooklyn Heights
I found myself in a pool of colored light

pouring out a stained-glass parlor window
on Joralemon Street. Behind it,

a piano playing Bach, muffled
talk, cocktails, social introductions

to smart handsome women, the kind
we find in Edith Wharton novels,

and soon I forgot whether I was walking
to or from my studio apartment.

I always dreamed of living in a place
where everyone would envy me, my wife,

the tunes I'd hum as I went out for mail.
In *Rear Window*, I never understood

why Jimmy Stewart is so obsessed
with everybody else's apartment

when he has Grace Kelly in *his*—
barely giving her a sidelong glance

as she passes him the telephoto lens
to satisfy his curiosity about

Raymond Burr's dumpy wife. Seriously,
I'd mind my business, if I had business

with a stunning blond in a party dress.